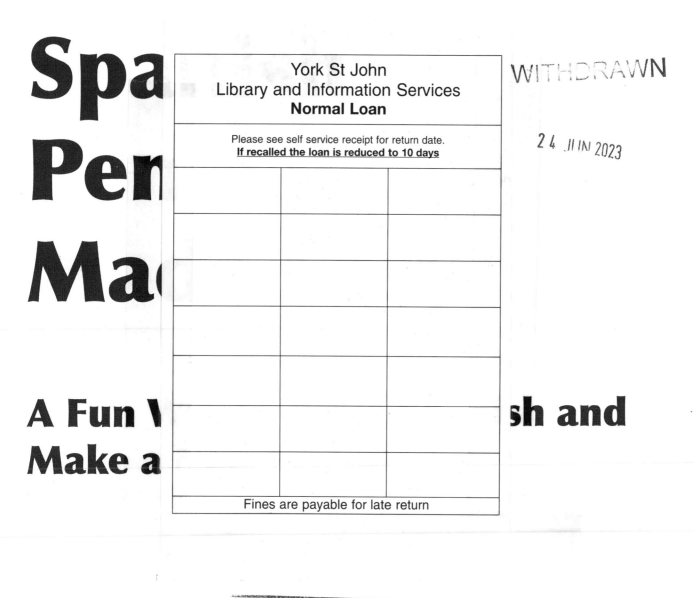

Spa
Pen
Ma

A Fun V sh and Make a

Sinéad Leleu and Belén de Vicente Fisher

Brilliant Publications

Dedication

For Chris Fisher, thanking you for all your help and support. BVF

We hope you and your pupils enjoy corresponding with your Spanish pen pals using this book. Brilliant Publications publishes many other books for teaching modern foreign languages. To find out more details on any of the titles listed below, please log onto our website: www.brilliantpublications.co.uk.

100+ Fun Ideas for Practising Modern Foreign Languages in the Primary Classroom	978-1-903853-98-6
¡Es Español!	978-1-903853-64-1
Juguemos Todos Juntos	978-1-903853-95-5
¡Vamos a Cantar!	978-1-905780-13-6
Chantez Plus Fort!	978-1-903853-37-5
Hexagonie 1	978-1-903853-92-4
Jouons Tous Ensemble	978-1-903853-81-8
C'est Français!	978-1-903853-02-3
J'aime Chanter!	978-1-905780-11-2
J'aime Parler!	978-1-905780-12-9
French Pen Pals Made Easy	978-1-905780-10-5
Das ist Deutsch	978-1-905780-15-0
Wir Spielen Zusammen	978-1-903853-97-9
German Pen Pals Made Easy	978-1-905780-43-3
Giochiamo Tutti Insieme	978-1-903853-96-2

Published by Brilliant Publications
Unit 10
Sparrow Hall Farm
Edlesborough
Dunstable
Bedfordshire
LU6 2ES, UK

Sales and stock enquiries:
Tel: 01202 712910
Fax: 0845 1309300
E-mail: brilliant@bebc.co.uk
Website: www.brilliantpublications.co.uk

General information enquiries:
Tel: 01525 222292

The name Brilliant Publications and the logo are registered trademarks.

Written by Sinéad Leleu and Belén de Vicente Fisher
Illustrated by James Walmesley
Front cover designed by Gloss Solutions

ISBN 978-1-905780-42-6

First printed and published in the UK in 2008

Contents

Introduction

In this era of technology, we MFL teachers are spoilt with an excellent array of resource material. Interactive CD-Roms, DVDs, Internet sites ... you name it, we use them all. The main aim of all this is that, one day, our pupils will be able to communicate with other MFL speakers through our chosen language. In my own classes, this 'one day' is now. This we do through pen pal correspondence.

My experience has shown me that, despite regularly introducing a variety of resources into my classes, rarely a class begins without a pupil asking 'Have our letters arrived yet?' 'No, todavía, no' is met with disappointment whereas 'Sí' is met with great excitement and delight. My pupils are unwaveringly eager to reply. This may seem like a daunting task to the less confident or the time-strapped teacher but ...

For the teacher, *Spanish Pen Pals Made Easy*:
- ◆ Does not require fluency
- ◆ Is time-saving – little or no preparation is required
- ◆ Links with the KS2 Framework for language teaching
- ◆ Has inherent cross-curricular links to geography, art and ICT
- ◆ Supplements, consolidates and revises course work.

For the pupil, *Spanish Pen Pals Made Easy*:
- ◆ Is easy to follow. The method used is gap-filling as opposed to giving pupils the daunting task of beginning with a blank page
- ◆ Is realistic. The pupil realizes that Spanish can be used for real-life communication and not just in an artificial situation
- ◆ Instils confidence. They can communicate effectively at a basic level
- ◆ Helps foster positive attitudes towards foreign language learning
- ◆ Facilitates intercultural understanding. The pupil can learn about Spanish culture through a Spanish peer
- ◆ ... and, of course, it is fun and a wonderful way to make a new friend. (I should know as I have had the same two pen pals for over 25 years!)

Spanish Pen Pals Made Easy
© Sinéad Leleu, Belén de Vicente Fisher and Brilliant Publications

Tips for the teacher

Where to find pen pals

1. There are many websites to help you to find a Spanish-speaking class to correspond with, for example:
   - www.epals.com
   - www.globalgateway.org
   - www.etwinning.net
   - www.ipf.net.au (small fee)

   If you have the option of choosing a country, do not forget other countries where you can find Spanish-speaking schools such as Mexico, Peru, Chile and Argentina.

2. If your town is twinned with a Spanish town, you could contact their 'Colegio de Educación Primaria' (ages 6–12) or 'Colegio de Educación Secundaria' (ages 12–18).

Checklist for you and your Spanish-speaking counterpart

1. Confirm with your Spanish-speaking counterpart that your pupils will write in Spanish and decide whether the replies will be in English or Spanish. (They may like to know that *Spanish Pen Pals Made Easy* can be purchased from Amazon.)
2. Decide which class will write first.
3. Decide how you are going to pair the pupils. Either one of the teachers decides or the pupils in the class that receives the first letters decide. It is a good idea to make a note of the pairs immediately as some pupils will not remember their pen pal's name. Unless you find a class with the exact same number of pupils, some pupils will have to write two letters.
4. Discuss the expected frequency of your letters. This depends on the school calendar, workload and enthusiasm. Be careful to decide on realistic deadlines. It is a good idea to take one term at a time.
5. Agree on the themes for the term ahead. Take into consideration seasonal events such as Christmas, Hallowe'en and local festivals.

Before pupils begin

1. Before pupils begin to write a letter, it is paramount to have covered the relevant language orally. Remember: **hear it, say it, see it, write it**.

2. Introduce letter writing with a sample letter written on the board, chart or overhead projector. You could use the letter for Unit 1, 'Déjame presentarme', on page 10; this letter can also be downloaded from our website so you can display it on a whiteboard: www.brilliantpublications.co.uk/PAGE1042_sample letter.pdf.

Highlight the five main parts of the letter:
- ◆ the heading, which includes the town and date
- ◆ the greeting
- ◆ the body of the letter
- ◆ the closing greeting
- ◆ the signature.

3. Before pupils begin their first letter, explain to them how to use *Spanish Pen Pals Made Easy*:
- ◆ Point out that pupils must first fill in the blanks and circle where there is a choice.
- ◆ Using imaginary details or those of a pupil in the class, go through the letter line by line. Complete and circle where necessary. See what pupils can come up with themselves before referring to the 'Vocabulario adicional' section.
- ◆ Write out the entire letter on the board. Explain to pupils that they will need to write a draft into their Spanish workbooks.
- ◆ Tell pupils that you will then correct their draft letters before they write their final letters.

Writing your first letter

1. Having explained how to use *Spanish Pen Pals Made Easy*, give each pupil the Spanish template letter for 'Déjame presentarme' (page 10). Depending on the class level and time, some teachers will prefer to only give certain sections of the unit. For example, if your class has a good level of Spanish, you may prefer not to hand out the English template. However, if unfinished letters are given as homework, it is advisable to give all four pages of the unit. As the templates and vocabulary are bilingual, parents/guardians will feel comfortable helping.

2. If you give out the English template, point out to your pupils that they are not always word-for-word translations. It is the ideas that are translated.

3. Once you have corrected the pupils' drafts, they should write their letters out neatly to send to their pen pals. Using personalized stationery can help to make their letters special. Allow the pupils to choose this for themselves.

4. If pupils wish to include enclosures such as postcards, photos, drawings etc, make sure that they are either stapled or stuck to the letter or that each pupil has their own individual envelope.

As you move on

1. As soon as you receive your first replies, get your pupils to stick their letters into their Spanish workbooks or put them into their Spanish folders.

2. *Spanish Pen Pals Made Easy* is flexible, so, excepting the first unit (Déjame presentarme), the units may be used in any order.

3. At the beginning of the correspondence, it will be easier for pupils to stick to the template letter. However, as many pupils become more competent, encourage them to change the order of the body of the letter. Weaker pupils can continue to stick to the template letter whereas stronger pupils can use the template letter as a 'springboard'.

4. You can give the class as a whole a choice of topics to choose from. Alternate the choice between the two corresponding classes.

5. To vary the correspondence, you could use other means, such as recorded messages on CD, tape, DVD or video.

6. Do not allow pupils to give their home address or telephone number (or e-mail if you are using snail mail) until the correspondence is well established.

Class projects

Class projects are an excellent way to vary class correspondence. The units 'Mi colegio', '¡Yo vivo!' and '¡La Navidad aquí!' are particularly suitable. The projects can be done in English with an English-Spanish glossary. The class can be divided into small groups and given one section each. Include drawings, photos, posters, videos, DVDs, CDs, brochures etc. A class project can be sent along with individual letters or in the place of individual letters. If you have any festivals particular to where you live, this would also be interesting for your pen pals.

Here are some ideas for things that could be included in the class projects:

Mi colegio
- ◆ our class timetable
- ◆ after-school activities
- ◆ school dinners
- ◆ our uniform
- ◆ our school building
- ◆ our teachers
- ◆ our school crest
- ◆ history of our school

¡Yo vivo!
- ◆ history
- ◆ a map
- ◆ landmark(s)
- ◆ festivals and celebrations
- ◆ clubs/activities for children
- ◆ food specialities
- ◆ local heroes and/or famous people
- ◆ traditional music
- ◆ languages and dialect

¡La Navidad aquí!
- ◆ Christmas food
- ◆ Christmas tree and decorations
- ◆ Christmas crackers
- ◆ A typical Christmas carol
- ◆ Christmas card-giving tradition
- ◆ Christmas stockings and gift-offering tradition
- ◆ 12 Days of Christmas
- ◆ Pantomimes

Classroom ideas

1. As soon as you receive your first replies, set up a 'pen pal corner' in your classroom. You can include a map of Europe, the world or the country of your pen pals, indicating where they live. You can also make flags of their country and your country. As the correspondence moves along, you can include anything that you or the pupils find interesting, such as traditional dishes, school brochures or festivals.

2. To work on oracy skills, pupils can give an oral presentation on their pen pal.

3. As part of art or ICT, pupils can make information sheets based on their pen pals with headings such as:
   - ◆ nombre
   - ◆ edad
   - ◆ ciudad
   - ◆ cumpleaños
   - ◆ color de ojos
   - ◆ color de pelo
   - ◆ hermanos y hermanas
   - ◆ animales / animal favorito
   - ◆ hobbies o pasatiempos
   - ◆ color favorito
   - ◆ música favorita
   - ◆ comida favorita
   - ◆ bebida favorita
   - ◆ asignatura favorita
   - ◆ estación favorita

Spanish Pen Pals Made Easy
© *Sinéad Leleu, Belén de Vicente Fisher and Brilliant Publications*

Tips for the pupil

1. Using a model letter, fill in the blanks and circle the words you would like to use. Check out the **'Vocabulario adicional'** (Extra vocabulary) section for extra vocabulary. You can keep the English translation nearby to help you.

2. Write out a draft letter (a practice letter). Your teacher will then correct it.

3. Rewrite a final copy of your letter.

4. To make your letter more interesting, use nice stationery and/or decorate your letter with colourful designs and drawings. You can use some of the ideas in the **'¡Ideas adicionales!'** (Extra ideas!) section.

5. Enclose anything you think may interest your pen pal such as stickers, magazine cuttings, and postcards. Again, you will find ideas in the **'¡Ideas adicionales!'** (Extra ideas!) section.

6. **Do not** give your home address, telephone number or home e-mail address without the permission of your parents and teacher.

7. Have fun!

¡Déjame presentarme!

_____   _____
(pueblo/ciudad)   (fecha)

¡Hola!

Me llamo _____ .

Tengo _____ años. ¿Cuántos años tienes tú?

Vivo en _____ , en _____ .
¿Dónde vives tú?   (tu país)

Soy una chica / Soy un chico.

Me gusta _____ y _____ .

No me gusta _____ .

¡Hasta pronto!

_____
(tu nombre)

_____
(town/village)

_____
(date)

Hello!

My name is _____ .

I'm _____ years old. How old are you?

I live in _____ , in _____ .
                                              (your country)
Where do you live?

I'm a girl. / I'm a boy.

I like _____ and _____ .

I don't like _____ .

Bye for now!

_____
(your first name)

Vocabulario adicional
Extra vocabulary

el fútbol	football	la música rock	rock music
los deportes	sports	la música clásica	classical music
el baile	dancing	el colegio	school
el baloncesto	basketball	el cine	the cinema
montar a caballo	horse riding	las películas de miedo (de terror)	horror movies
la natación	swimming	la moda	fashion
el atletismo	athletics	el teatro	drama/theatre
		los Simpsons	The Simpsons

el chocolate	chocolate	(en) Francia	(in) France
los caramelos	sweets	(en) Inglaterra	(in) England
la coca cola	cola	(en) Escocia	(in) Scotland
el brócoli	broccoli	(en) Gales	(in) Wales
la pizza	pizza	(en) Irlanda	(in) Ireland
las espinacas	spinach		
las coles de Bruselas	Brussels sprouts		
el helado	ice cream		

Puntos adicionales
Extra points

1. Boy or girl?
Your pen pal may not know from your first name if you are a girl or a boy. So, it's a good idea to tell them.

2. Tengo 10 años
Did you notice that, to say how old we are in Spanish, we say '*¡Tengo 10 años!*' This literally means 'I have 10 years'!

3. El, la, los, las

In English we say:	but in Spanish we say:
I like football.	Me gusta **el** fútbol.
I like classical music.	Me gusta **la** música clásica.
I like sweets.	Me gustan **los** caramelos.
I like horror movies	Me gustan **las** películas de miedo.

el
la   } the
los
las

El means 'the' before a masculine word such as:

el queso	the cheese
el brócoli	the broccoli
el zumo de naranja	the orange juice

La means 'the' before a feminine word such as:

la música clásica	the classical music
la manzana	the apple
la coca	the cola

Los means 'the' before a masculine word in the plural such as:

los deportes	the sports
los Simpsons	The Simpsons
los caramelos	the sweets

Las means 'the' before a feminine word in the plural such as:

las pizzas	the pizzas
las mazanas	the apples
las películas de miedo	horror movies

¡Ideas adicionales!
Extra ideas!

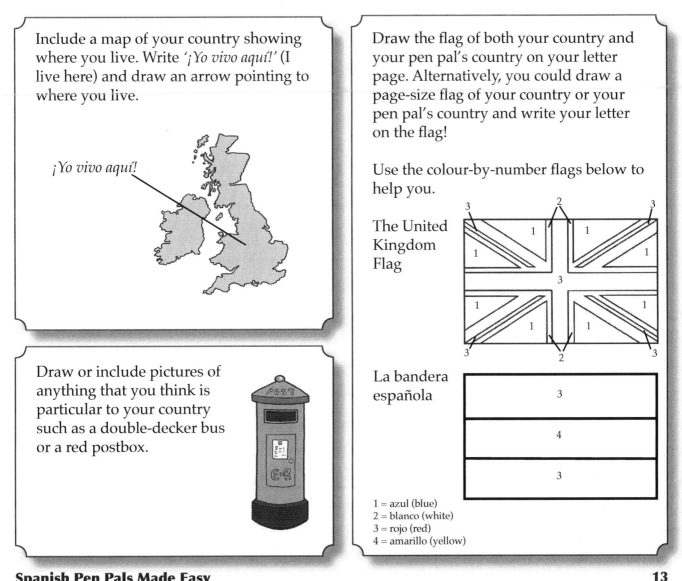

Include a map of your country showing where you live. Write '*¡Yo vivo aquí!*' (I live here) and draw an arrow pointing to where you live.

¡Yo vivo aquí!

Draw or include pictures of anything that you think is particular to your country such as a double-decker bus or a red postbox.

Draw the flag of both your country and your pen pal's country on your letter page. Alternatively, you could draw a page-size flag of your country or your pen pal's country and write your letter on the flag!

Use the colour-by-number flags below to help you.

The United Kingdom Flag

La bandera española

1 = azul (blue)
2 = blanco (white)
3 = rojo (red)
4 = amarillo (yellow)

_____ _____
(pueblo/ciudad)   (fecha)

Querido/querida _____ / ¡Hola!

Gracias por tu carta.

¿Qué tal? Yo _____ .

Tengo los ojos _____ y el pelo

_____ .

Soy _____ y _____ .
        (adjetivo)   (adjetivo)

Mi cumpleaños es el _____ de _____ .
¿Cuándo es tu cumpleaños?

Mi color favorito es el _____ . ¿Y el tuyo?
¿Cuál es tu color favorito?

¡Escríbeme pronto!
¡Adiós!

_____
(tu nombre)

Spanish Pen Pals Made Easy
© Sinéad Leleu, Belén de Vicente Fisher and Brilliant Publications

_____
(town/village)

_____
(date)

Dear _____ / Hello!

Thank you for your letter.

How are you? I'm _____ .

I have _____ eyes and _____ hair.

I'm _____ and _____ .
(adjective)   (adjective)

My birthday is the _____ of _____.
When is your birthday?

My favourite colour is _____. How about you?
What's your favourite colour?

Write soon!
Bye!

_____
(your first name)

Vocabulario adicional
Extra vocabulary

bien	well/fine
muy bien	very well
mal	not well
hola / adiós	hi there / bye

azul	blue
gris	grey
verde	green
amarillo	yellow
marrón	brown
rosa	pink
naranja	orange
morado	purple
negro	black
rojo	red
blanco	white

enero	January
febrero	February
marzo	March
abril	April
mayo	May
junio	June
julio	July
agosto	August
septiembre	September
octubre	October
noviembre	November
diciembre	December

claro	light
oscuro	dark
largo	long
corto	short
rizado	curly
liso	straight

bonito	nice
gracioso	funny
simpático	friendly
sensible	sensitive
tímido	shy

Tengo los ojos …
azules	blue
verdes	green
marrones	brown
grises	grey
castaños	hazel

Tengo el pelo …
rubio	blonde/fair
castaño claro	light brown
castaño oscuro	dark brown
negro	black
Soy pelirrojo(a)	I have red hair

Puntos adicionales
Extra points

1. Describing your eyes
In English, we say 'I have green eyes'. The colour comes before the word 'eyes'. Did you notice that in Spanish the colour comes after the word *'ojos'*? So, *'Tengo los ojos verdes'*. As *'ojos'* is plural, we must also make the colour plural. This is usually done by adding *'s'*.

2. Describing your hair
When describing your hair colour you also put the colour after the word. In English, we say 'I have black hair'. In Spanish, we say *'Tengo el pelo negro'*. If you want to add a second adjective to describe your hair, you say *'Tengo el pelo negro y rizado'* ('I have black curly hair').

Spanish Pen Pals Made Easy
© Sinéad Leleu, Belén de Vicente Fisher and Brilliant Publications

3. Writing dates

In English, we write the months with a capital letter, eg the 15th of November. In Spanish, we write the months with a small letter, eg *el 15 de noviembre*.

4. Colours

When we are saying our favourite colour, we must put *'el'* before the colour, *'Mi color favorito es el _____'*.

¡Ideas adicionales!
Extra ideas!

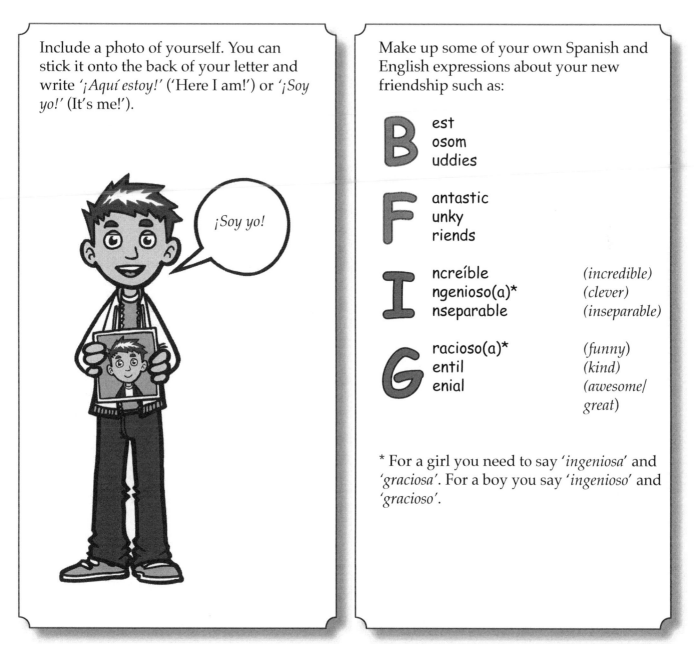

Include a photo of yourself. You can stick it onto the back of your letter and write *'¡Aquí estoy!'* ('Here I am!') or *'¡Soy yo!'* (It's me!').

¡Soy yo!

Make up some of your own Spanish and English expressions about your new friendship such as:

B est
      osom
      uddies

F antastic
      unky
      riends

I ncreíble   (incredible)
      ngenioso(a)*   (clever)
      nseparable   (inseparable)

G racioso(a)*   (funny)
      entil   (kind)
      enial   (awesome/
                        great)

* For a girl you need to say *'ingeniosa'* and *'graciosa'*. For a boy you say *'ingenioso'* and *'gracioso'*.

_____   _____
(pueblo/ciudad)   (fecha)

Querido / querida _____ / ¡Hola!

Gracias por tu carta y foto. ¿Qué tal estás?

Yo bien / muy bien / mal.

Tengo _____ hermana(s) y _____ hermano(s).

Mi hermana se llama _____ . Tiene _____ años. /

Mi hermano se llama _____ . Tiene _____ años. /

Soy hijo único / soy hija única.

¿Tú tienes hermanos y hermanas?

Tengo un /una _____ que se llama _____ .
                (animal)

Él / ella es _____ .
             (adjetivo)

¿Tú tienes mascotas?

Yo no tengo mascotas, pero mi animal favorito es el /la

_____ .
   (animal)

¡Escríbeme pronto!

¡Hablamos pronto! / ¡Adiós!

_____
    (tu nombre)

Spanish Pen Pals Made Easy
© Sinéad Leleu, Belén de Vicente Fisher and Brilliant Publications

_____
(town/village)

_____
(date)

Dear _____ / Hello!

Thank you for your letter and your photo.

How are you ? I'm fine / very well / not well.

I have ___ sister(s) and ___ brother(s).

My sister's name is _____ . She is ___ years old. /

My brother's name is _____ . He is ___ years old. /

I'm an only child.

Do you have brothers and sisters?

I have a _____ who is called _____ .
      (animal)

He / she is _____ .
       (adjective)

Do you have a pet?

I don't have a pet, but my favourite animal is the

_____ .
(animal)

Write soon!

Talk soon! / Bye!

_____
(your first name)

© Sinéad Leleu, Belén de Vicente Fisher and Brilliant Publications

Vocabulario adicional
Extra vocabulary

Aquí está …	Here is …
Tú eres …	You are …
Soy yo	This is me / It's me

un gato	a cat
un perro	a dog
un pez	a fish
un conejo	a rabbit
un hamster	a hamster
un pájaro	a bird
un ratón	a mouse
un caballo	a horse
una cobaya	a guinea pig

mi padre	my father
mi papá	my dad
mi madre	my mother
mi mamá	my mum
mi madrastra	my step-mother
mi padrastro	my step-father
mi hermanastro	my step-brother
mi hermanastra	my step-sister
mi abuela	my grandmother
mi abuelo	my grandfather
mis padres adoptivos	my foster parents

dulce	sweet
gracioso(a)	funny
irritante	annoying
adorable	adorable
juguetón(ona)	playful

Puntos adicionales
Extra points

1. Types of family

There are many types of family. If you live with your grandparents or foster parents or anybody else, you can say *'Vivo con _____'* (I live with _____).

2. Dear …

If your pen pal is a boy, you must translate 'Dear' to *'Querido'*. If your pen pal is a girl, you must translate 'Dear' to *'Querida'*.

3. More than one brother and sister

For more than one brother, you can say:

> *Mis hermanos se llaman _____ y _____ .*
> (My brothers' names are _____ and _____ .)

The same applies for more than one sister:

> *Mis hermanas se llaman _____ y _____ .*
> (My sisters' names are _____ and _____ .)

Spanish Pen Pals Made Easy
© Sinéad Leleu, Belén de Vicente Fisher and Brilliant Publications

4. More than one pet

If you have more than one pet, you can say:

Tengo 2 perros que se llaman _____ y _____ .
(I have 2 dogs who are called _____ and _____.)

Don't forget to make the animal plural. Most words are made plural by adding 's', such as:

Tengo 2 ratones, 3 conejos y 4 gatos
(I have 2 mice, 3 rabbits and 4 cats.)

The plural of '*pez*' (fish) is '*peces*'.

Tengo 2 peces.
(I have 2 fish.)

If you would like to describe your pets, then it is easiest to describe each pet individually:

Tengo 2 perros que se llaman Max y Molly. Max es juguetón. Molly es adorable.
(I have 2 dogs called Max and Molly. Max is playful. Molly is adorable.)

5. Mi, mis

In Spanish, there are two ways to say 'my':

mi
mis } my

If the noun is singular, we use '*mi*':

If the noun is plural, we use '*mis*':

mi hermano	my brother
mi hermana	my sister
mis hermanos	my brothers
mis hermanas	my sisters

¡Ideas adicionales!
Extra ideas!

Include photos of your family. You could stick a photo to the back of your letter. Draw a frame around your photo. Write '*Soy yo*' and use an arrow to point to yourself. For other members of your family, write '*Es mi hermano*' or '*Es mi padrastro*' etc and use arrows to point to the person in the photo.

Es mi padre.   *Es mi madre.*

Es mi hermano.

Soy yo.

_____   _____
(pueblo/ciudad)   (fecha)

Querido / Querida _____ / ¡Hola!

Gracias por tu carta / tu foto / tus fotos.
¿Qué tal estás? / ¿Qué tal? Yo bien.

¿Tienes algún hobby? Yo juego al _____ /
yo hago _____ .

Me encanta _____ porque es divertido/ relajante/
interesante/ energético/ un deporte en grupo. ¿Y tú?
¿A ti qué te gusta?

Colecciono _____ .
De momento estoy leyendo '_____'.
Me gustaría aprender a _____ .

En mi colegio el hobbie más popular es el _____ .
¿Y tú?

¡Escríbeme pronto!
¡Hablamos pronto! / Tu amigo / amiga,

_____
(tu nombre)

© Sinéad Leleu, Belén de Vicente Fisher and Brilliant Publications

_____
(town/village)

_____
(date)

Hi there / Dear _____ ,

Thank you for your letter / your photo / your photos.
How are you? / How are you? I'm fine.

Do you have hobbies? I play _____ /
I do _____ .

I love _____ because it's fun / relaxing / interesting /
energetic / a team sport. How about you? What do you like?

I collect _____ .
At the moment, I'm reading '_____'.
I would like to learn to _____ .

In my school, the most popular hobby is _____ .
How about you?

Write soon!
Talk soon! / Your friend,

_____
(your first name)

Vocabulario adicional

Extra vocabulary

toco el piano	I play the piano
toco el violín	I play the violin
toco la flauta traversera	I play the flute
toco la guitarra	I play the guitar

juego al fútbol	I play football
juego al baloncesto	I play basketball
juego al rugby	I play rugby
juego al voleibol	I play volleyball
juego al hockey	I play hockey
juego al golf	I play golf

juego con mi consola / playstation	I play on my playstation
juego al ordenador	I play computer games
juego a la petanca	I play petanque (game similar to bowls)
hago ciclismo	I cycle
hago gimnasia	I do gymnastics
hago judo	I do judo
hago atletismo	I do athletics
hago karate	I do karate
hago equitación	I go horse riding

especialmente	especially
y	and
jugar	to play
hacer	to do
no me gusta	I don't like
odio	I hate
me gusta bastante	I quite like

nadando	swimming
leyendo	reading
bailando	dancing
nadar	to swim
leer	to read
bailar	to dance
el arte	art
el teatro	theatre
mirar la tele	to watch TV
escuchar música	to listen to music
ir al cine	to go to the cinema

los sellos	stamps
las muñecas	dolls
las pegatinas	stickers
las monedas	coins
los peluches	cuddly toys
las cartas _____	_____ cards

Puntos adicionales

Extra points

1. Sports

jugar a (+ un deporte) – to play (+ a sport)

In English, when we speak about playing sports we say 'I play football', 'I play volleyball', 'I play hockey', etc.

In Spanish, when the sport is a masculine word, we say:

Juego **al** futból.   I play football.

When the sport is a feminine word, we say:

Juego **a la** petanca.   I play petanque.

© Sinéad Leleu, Belén de Vicente Fisher and Brilliant Publications

2. Musical instruments

toco (un instrumento musical) – to play (a musical instrument)

When we speak about playing musical instruments, we say 'I play the piano', I play the guitar', 'I play the violin', etc.

In Spanish when the musical instrument is a masculine word, we say:

Toco **el** piano.   I play the piano.

When the musical instrument is feminine, we say:

Toco **la** guitarra.   I play the guitar.

3. Me gusta ... – I like ...

You can use the noun or the verb to say you like something:

Me gusta la natación.   or   Me gusta nadar.
Me gusta la lectura.   or   Me gusta leer.
Me gusta el fútbol.   or   Me gusta jugar al fútbol.
Me gusta el piano.   or   Me gusta tocar el piano.
Me gusta el judo.   or   Me gusta hacer judo.

¡Ideas adicionales!
Extra ideas!

Include drawings, photos or magazine cuttings of anything to do with your hobbies, eg your favourite football team, your favourite singers or you practising a hobby.

If you are interested in sports, here is a football chant for the Spanish Real Madrid team:
¡Hala Madrid, hala Madrid, el equipo campeón de primera división, hala Madrid, hala Madrid, hala Madrid!

_____ _____
(pueblo/ciudad)   *(fecha)*

Querido / Querida _____ / ¡Hola!

Gracias por tu carta./ Me puse muy contento/a al recibir tu carta.
¿Qué tal estás? Yo bien/ muy bien/ genial.

Mi colegio se llama _____ . Es
un internado mixto/ de chicas/ de chicos. Estoy en el curso
_____ y hay _____ niños en mi clase. Mi profesor
                   (número)
/ Mi profesora se llama _____ . Él /ella es
_____ .
        (adjetivo)

Llevo uniforme. / No llevo uniforme. ¿Y tú?

Curso _____ asignaturas: _____
      (número)   *(tus asignaturas)*
.
Mi asignatura favorita es _____ porque es
_____ . No me gusta _____
porque es _____ . ¿Cuál es tu asignatura favorita?

¡Escríbeme pronto!
¡Hasta pronto! / ¡Adiós!

_____
(tu nombre)

© Sinéad Leleu, Belén de Vicente Fisher and Brilliant Publications

_____
(town/village)

_____
(date)

Dear _____ / Hello!

Thank you for your letter. / I was very happy to get your letter.
How are you? I'm fine / very well / great.

My school is called _____ . It's a
mixed / girls' / boys' / boarding school. I'm in year _____
and there are _____ in my class. My teacher's
        (number)
name is _____ . He / She is

_____ .
        (adjective)

I wear a uniform. / I don't wear a uniform. How about you?

I do _____ subjects: _____ .
      (number)   (your subjects)
My favourite subject is _____ because it's
_____ . I don't like _____
because it's _____ . What's your favourite subject?

Write soon!
Goodbye! / Bye!

_____
(your first name)

Vocabulario adicional
Extra vocabulary

me encanta	I love
lo odio	I hate
el recreo	break-time
comida	lunch
(a mediodía)	

lunes	Monday
martes	Tuesday
miércoles	Wednesday
jueves	Thursday
viernes	Friday
sábado	Saturday
domingo	Sunday

las matemáticas	mathematics
la lengua	language
la historia	history
la geografía	geography
la música	music
la educación física	PE
la educación plástica	art and design
las ciencias	science
el español	Spanish
el inglés	English
la educación para la cuidadanía	citizenship
la informática	ICT

porque	because
es	it's
interesante	interesting
aburrido(a)	boring
difícil	difficult
fácil	easy
bueno(a)	nice
estricto(a)	strict
gracioso(a)	funny
y	and

Puntos adicionales
Extra points

1. Spanish and British schools

Spanish and British schools have different names for the school years. Find the equivalent for your year.

Colegio de Educación Primaria – Primary School

Spain	UK	Age
Segundo de Primaria	Year 2	7–8
Tercero de Primaria	Year 3	8–9
Cuarto de Primaria	Year 4	9–10
Quinto de Primaria	Year 5	10–11
Sexto de Primaria	Year 6	11–12

Colegio de Educación Secundaria – Secondary School

Spain	UK	Age
1º de la ESO*	Year 7	12–13
2º de la ESO*	Year 8	13–14
3º de la ESO*	Year 9	14–15
4º de la ESO*	Year 10	15–16

*ESO = Educación Secundaria Obligatoria

2. Teacher

'*Profesor*' is used for male teachers. '*Profesora*' is used for female teachers.

Spanish Pen Pals Made Easy
© Sinéad Leleu, Belén de Vicente Fisher and Brilliant Publications

3. Feminine adjectives

If you are describing a girl or woman, you must make the adjective feminine by changing the '*o*' at the end of the adjective to an '*a*'.

Él es estrict**o**. / Ella es estrict**a**.   He is strict. / She is strict.

If the adjective already ends with an '*e*', we do not add an extra '*e*'.

Él es interesante. / Ella es interesante.   He is interesting. / She is interesting.

'Fácil' and 'difícil' stay the same for both masculine and feminine.

4. Tu, tus

In Spanish, there are two ways to say 'your':

tu
tus   } your

If the noun is singular, we use '*tu*':   **tu desayuno**   your breakfast
If the noun is plural, we use '*tus*':   **tus profesores**   your teachers

¡Ideas adicionales!

Extra ideas!

Include your own timetable. Write each subject in a different colour. If you don't have a timetable, ask your teacher. Here is an example from a Spanish school to help you do your own: '*Aquí está mi horario*' ('Here is my timetable').

Horas	Lunes	Martes	Miércoles	Jueves	Viernes
9 h – 10 h	Lengua	Matemáticas	Lengua	Matemáticas	Lengua
10 h - 11 h	Inglés	Ed. Física	Matemáticas	Inglés	Ed. Física
11 h – 11,45 h	Cto. Medio	Ed. para la Ciudadanía	Inglés	Lengua	Cto. Medio
Recreo					
12,15 h – 13,15 h	Matemáticas	Lengua	Informática	Música	Matemáticas
13,15 h – 14 h	Cto. Medio	Cto. Medio	Ed. para la Ciudadanía	Cto. Medio	Plástica

Cto. Medio stands for '*Conocimento del Medio*', which roughly translates as 'knowledge of the world'. It includes science, geography and history.

_____   _____
(pueblo/ciudad)   (fecha)

Querido / Querida _____ / ¡Hola!

Gracias por tu carta. / Me puse muy contento/a al recibir tu carta.
Espero que estés bien. Yo estoy bien / más o menos / genial.

¿Tú qué comes? A mí me gusta _____ y

_____ . No me gusta _____ .

¿Qué te gusta beber? A mí me gusta _____

y_____ .
No me gusta _____ .

Aquí en _____ , '_____'
                        (tu país)
es un plato tradicional.

¡Escríbeme pronto!
Tu amigo / amiga,

_____
(tu nombre)

© Sinéad Leleu, Belén de Vicente Fisher and Brilliant Publications

_____
(town/village)

_____
(date)

Dear _____ / Hello!

Thank you for your letter. / I was very happy to get your letter.
I hope you are well. I'm fine / not bad / great.

What do you eat? I like _____ and
_____ .

I don't like _____ .

What do you like to drink? I like _____ and
_____ .

I don't like _____ .

Here in _____ , '_____'
           (your country)
is a traditional dish.

Write soon!
Your friend,

_____
(your first name)

Vocabulario adicional
Extra vocabulary

el café	coffee
el té	tea
la coca cola	cola
el zumo de naranja	orange juice
la leche	milk
el agua	water
el chocolate caliente	hot chocolate

el helado de vainilla	vanilla ice-cream
el helado de caramelo	caramel ice-cream
el helado de fresa	strawberry ice-cream
los caramelos	sweets
los crepes	pancakes
la tarta	cake
el chocolate	chocolate

la piña	pineapple
la frambuesa	raspberry
la naranja	orange
las uvas	grapes
el plátano	banana
la manzana	apple
las pasas	raisins

el sándwich de queso	cheese sandwich
el sándwich de jamón	ham sandwich
el puré de patatas	mashed potatoes
la tortilla francesa	omelette
la sopa	soup
las patatas fritas	chips / crisps
la pizza	pizza
el quiche	quiche
la hamburguesa	burger

las patatas	potatoes
la zanahoria	carrot
el brócoli	broccoli
las espinacas	spinach
la ensalada	salad
las coles de Bruselas	Brussels sprouts

me encanta	I love
me gusta bastante	I quite like
lo odio	I hate
¡Mmm!	Yum, yum!
¡Egh!	Yuck!

Spanish Pen Pals Made Easy
© Sinéad Leleu, Belén de Vicente Fisher and Brilliant Publications

Puntos adicionales
Extra points

1. Your friend
'*Tu amigo*' or '*tu amiga*'? If you are talking about a boy, you say '*tu amigo*'. If you are talking about a girl, you say '*tu amiga*'. We change the '*o*' at the end to an '*a*' to make '*amigo*' feminine.

2. Spanish dishes
The following are examples of traditional Spanish dishes:
* Paella
* Calamares
* Tortilla de patatas
* Torrijas
* Ajo blanco
* Gazpacho

¡Ideas adicionales!
Extra ideas!

Include the recipe for the traditional dish you have chosen. You can write this in English, but look up the ingredients in a bilingual dictionary and include a mini-glossary.

Design your perfect menu. Put it on the back of your letter. Use the example below to help you.

¡Aquí está el menú ideal!
(Here is the ideal menu!)

Menú de
_____
(tu nombre)

Lomo con patatas
o
Puré de patatas y salchichas

Coca cola
o
Zumo de naranja

Helado de chocolate
o
Helado de vainilla

_____   _____
(pueblo/ciudad)   (fecha)

Querido / Querida _____ / ¡ Hola!

Estaba encantado/a al recibir tu carta. Muchísimas gracias.
¿Qué tal estás? Yo estoy bien / muy bien.

¿Qué tal tu día? Yo me despierto a la/las _____ . ¿A qué
hora te despiertas tú? El colegio empieza a la/las _____.
¿Y tu colegio?

Como a la/las _____ y acabo el colegio a la/las _____. ¿Y tú?

Ceno a la/las _____ y me voy a la cama a las
_____. ¿A qué hora te vas a dormir tú?

¿Cuál es tu estación del año favorita? Mi estación favorita es
_____ porque me encanta _____ y
cuando _____ .
                    (el tiempo)

¡Escríbeme pronto!
¡Hasta pronto! ¡Adiós!

_____
(tu nombre)

_____
(town/village)

_____
(date)

Hi there! / Dear _____ ,

I was delighted to get your letter. Thank you very much.
How are you? I'm fine / great.

How is your day? I get up at _____ a.m. What time do you get
up? School starts at _____ a.m. What about your school?

I have lunch at _____ p.m. and I leave school at
_____ p.m. How about you?

I have dinner at _____ and I go to bed at _____ .
What time do you go to bed?

What's your favourite season? My favourite season is
_____ because I love _____
and when it _____ .
                              (the weather)

Write soon!
Talk soon! / Bye!

_____
(your first name)

Vocabulario adicional
Extra vocabulary

yo tomo el desayuno	I eat breakfast
me voy de casa	I leave home
llego al colegio	I get to school
yo duermo	I sleep
yo hago actividades extracurriculares	I do after-school activities
yo veo la televisión / (tele)	I watch TV
yo leo	I read

primavera	spring
verano	summer
otoño	autumn
invierno	winter

hace bueno	it's fine
hace sol	it's sunny
está nevando	it's snowing
hace viento	it's windy
hace calor	it's hot
está lloviendo	it's raining
hace frío	it's cold

Navidad	Christmas
las vacaciones escolares	the school holidays
Halloween	Hallowe'en
Semana Santa	Easter holidays
mi cumpleaños	my birthday
ir a la playa	to go to the beach
los colores otoñales	autumn colours
los narcisos	the daffodils
hacer un muñeco de nieve	to make a snowman
tener una pelea de bolas de nieve	to have a snowball fight

Puntos adicionales
Extra points

Time

In English, we usually use a.m. and p.m. to differentiate between morning and evening. In Spanish, it is more common to use the 24 hour clock.

1 a.m. = 1h	7 a.m. = 7h	1 p.m. = 13h	7 p.m. = 19h
2 a.m. = 2h	8 a.m. = 8h	2 p.m. = 14h	8 p.m. = 20h
3 a.m. = 3h	9 a.m. = 9h	3 p.m. = 15h	9 p.m. = 21h
4 a.m. = 4h	10 a.m. = 10h	4 p.m. = 16h	10 p.m. = 22h
5 a.m. = 5h	11 a.m. = 11h	5 p.m. = 17h	11 p.m. = 23h
6 a.m. = 6h	12 p.m. = 12h	6 p.m. = 18h	12 a.m. = 24h

In Spanish, the minutes go after the h (the hour), so:

8.15 a.m. = 8h15

8.30 a.m. = 8h30

8.45 a.m. = 8h45

Spanish Pen Pals Made Easy

¡Ideas adicionales!
Extra ideas!

Fill in the times in the following daily routine.

Yo me despierto a la / las _____ .

Yo desayuno a la / las _____ .

Yo llego al colegio a la / las _____ .

Yo como a la / las _____ .

Yo salgo del colegio a la / las _____ .

Yo hago mis actividades a la / las _____

Yo ceno a la / las _____ .

Yo me duermo a la / las _____ .

To make your daily routine more interesting, why not add speech bubbles.
You could fill them with comments such as:

¡Está delicioso!
(It's delicious!)

¡Estoy cansado(a)!
(I'm tired!)

¡Estoy contento(a)!
(I'm happy!)

¡Llego tarde!
(I'm late!)

_____   _____
(pueblo/ciudad)   _(fecha)_

Querido / Querida _____ / ¡Hola!

¿Qué tal estás?

Yo bien, gracias. / Yo muy bien, gracias.

Vivo en _____ . Es un pueblo / una ciudad / Esta en

el campo. Es _____ . Hay _____
                            (adjetivo)

habitantes.

¿Cómo es tu pueblo / ciudad?

En _____ , hay una piscina / una biblioteca /
        (tu pueblo/ciudad)

un supermercado / un hospital / un ayuntamiento / un café / un

restaurante / un cine / un colegio / un parque / una farmacia / una

carnicería / una panadería / un castillo / un río / una iglesia.

Cada año en el mes de _____ , celebramos
                                    (costumbre/tradición)

_____ / tenemos un carnaval.

¿Y tú?

¡Escríbeme pronto!

¡Adiós!/ Tu amigo / amiga,

_____
(tu nombre)

© Sinéad Leleu, Belén de Vicente Fisher and Brilliant Publications

_____
(town/village)

_____
(date)

Hello / Dear _____ ,

How are you?

I'm fine, thanks. / I'm great, thanks.

I live in _____ . It's a village / a town / a city / in

the country. It's _____ . There are _____

_____(adjective)_____

inhabitants. What's your town / your village like?

In _____ , there is a swimming pool / a library /

_____(your town/ village)_____

a supermarket / a hospital / a town hall / a café / a restaurant / a

cinema / a school / a park / a pharmacy / a butcher / a bakery / a

castle / a river / a church.

Every year in the month of _____, we celebrate

_____ / we have a carnival.

_____(custom/tradition)_____

How about you?

Write soon!

Goodbye! / Bye! / Your friend,

_____
(your first name)

Vocabulario adicional
Extra vocabulary

un banco	a bank
un estadio	a stadium
una tienda	a shop
un museo	a museum
una oficina de correos	the post office
un mercado	a market
una pista de hielo	an ice rink
una calle	a street
una estación de tren	a train station
un aeropuerto	an airport
una fábrica	a factory

ocupado(a)	busy
grande	big
ruidoso(a)	noisy
bonito(a)	pretty
tranquilo	peaceful
pequeño(a)	small
precioso(a)	beautiful
majo(a)	nice
aburrido(a)	boring
animado(a)	lively

encima de	on
una isla	an island
en la playa	by the beach
cerca	near

una feria	a fair
El Año Nuevo chino	the Chinese New Year
Día de San Jorge	Saint George's Day
Martes de Carnaval	Pancake Day
Día de San Andrés	Saint Andrew's Day
Primero de mayo	May Day
Procesión de Semana Santa	Easter parade

Puntos adicionales
Extra points

1. Prepositions to describe where you live
You can give a clearer idea of where you live by using prepositions, for example:

Está cerca de Leeds / Manchester / Londres / Stonehenge.
(It's near Leeds / Manchester / London / Stonehenge.)

Está en la playa.
(It's by the beach.)

Está en una isla.
(It's on an island.)

Está en la Isla de _____.
(It's on the Isle of _____.)

Spanish Pen Pals Made Easy
© *Sinéad Leleu, Belén de Vicente Fisher and Brilliant Publications*

2. Adjectives

You can also use adjectives to describe buildings and public places. Adjectives go after the noun in Spanish. For example:

un museo bonito	a nice museum
una piscina pequeña	a small swimming pool
un estadio grande	a big stadium
una iglesia grande	a big church

3. Plurals

In Spanish, we usually put an 's' on the end of the noun to make it plural. For example:

Hay un restaurante.	There is a restaurant.
Hay restaurantes.	There are restaurants.
Hay una iglesia.	There is a church.
Hay iglesias.	There are churches.

4. Famous for anything?

If the area where you live is famous or known for anything such as a market, a sporting event, a famous person, a particular type of food or an historical event, you can say:

_____ *es conocido por* _____ .
     (tu ciudad)

(_____ is famous / known for _____ .)
     (your town)

¡Ideas adicionales!

Extra ideas!

Include tourist guides or brochures of your village/town/city or county.

Draw a plan of your town / village or an area of where you live. Label your plan in Spanish.

una iglesia *un colegio* *un parque* *¡Yo vivo aquí!*

_____   _____
                (pueblo/ciudad)   *(fecha)*

¡Hola! / Querido / Querida _____ ,

¿Qué tal estás? Yo Bien / no muy bien. Muchas gracias por tu carta.

¿Te gusta la moda? Adoro la moda / Odio la moda.

En el fin de semana, me gusta llevar _____ y

_____ . Me gusta la ropa _____ .
                                                    (adjetivo)

¿Y tú?

Llevo un uniforme al colegio. Es obligatorio. / No llevo uniforme.

¿Tú llevas uniforme?

Yo llevo un jersey _____ / un pantalón
                            (color)

_____ / una camisa _____ / una
      (color)   *(color)*

falda _____ / un vestido _____ / una corbata
       (color)   *(color)*

_____ / un chándal _____ / unos zapatos
  (color)   *(color)*

_____ .
  (color)

¿_____ , no?
           (adjetivo)

¡Escríbeme pronto!

Tu amigo(a) / ¡Hasta pronto! / Con amor,

_____
        (tu nombre)

Spanish Pen Pals Made Easy
© Sinéad Leleu, Belén de Vicente Fisher and Brilliant Publications

_____
(town/village)

_____
(date)

Hello / Dear _____ ,

How are you? I'm fine / not very well.
Thanks a lot for your letter.

Do you like fashion? I love /hate fashion.

At the weekend, I like to wear _____ and
_____ . I like _____ clothes. How about you?
                                      (adjective)

I wear a uniform to school. It's compulsory. / I don't wear a
uniform. Do you wear a uniform?

I wear a _____ jumper / _____ trousers / a
            (colour)   (colour)
_____ shirt / a _____ skirt / a
  (colour)   (colour)
_____ dress / a _____ tie / a
  (colour)   (colour)
_____ tracksuit / _____ shoes.
  (colour)   (colour)
_____ , isn't it?
            (adjective)

Write soon!
Your friend / Talk soon! / Love,

_____
        (your first name)

Vocabulario adicional
Extra vocabulary

grande	big		unos vaqueros	jeans
pequeño(a)	small		una camiseta	a T-shirt
largo(a)	long		un suéter	a sweater
corto(a)	short		unas zapatillas de	trainers
pasado(a) de moda	old-fashioned		deporte	
			un vestido	a dress
			una bufanda	a scarf
rojo(a)	red		una gorra de béisbol	a baseball cap
naranja	orange		una chaqueta	a jacket
amarillo(a)	yellow		un sombrero	a hat
verde	green		un abrigo	a coat
rosa	pink		una camisa	a shirt
azul	blue		un jersey	a jersey
morado(a)	purple			
negro(a)	black			
marrón	brown		a la moda	fashionable
blanco(a)	white		moderno(a)	trendy
gris	grey		elegante	smart
azul marino	navy		cómodo(a)	comfortable
			simple	simple
			de colores vivos	brightly coloured
			precioso(a)	lovely
			horrible	awful
			normalmente	usually
			a veces	sometimes

Puntos adicionales
Extra points

1. Adjective agreement

Colours are adjectives, so they need to agree with the noun they are describing.

If the noun is masculine, you need to use the masculine form of the colour:

un jersey **rojo**	a red jumper
un vestido **negro**	a black dress

If the noun is feminine, you need to use the feminine form of the colour:

una bufanda **roja**	a red scarf
una camisa **morada**	a purple shirt

© Sinéad Leleu, Belén de Vicente Fisher and Brilliant Publications

Note

Many colour words in Spanish stay the same, whether the word they are describing is masculine or feminine. For example:

un vestido naranja	an orange dress
una bufanda naranja	an orange scarf
un abrigo rosa	a pink coat
una camiseta rosa	a pink T-shirt

2. Plural

If the noun is plural, you must change the colour to its plural form:

dos pantalon**es** verd**es**	two pairs of green trousers
seis jersey**s** azul**es**	six blue jerseys
cuatro zapato**s** gris**es**	four grey shoes
unos zapato**s** negro**s**	some black shoes

¡Ideas adicionales!

Extra ideas!

Mi ropa favorita (My favourite outfit)

Draw your favourite outfit on your letter or include a photo of you wearing your favourite outfit, sports gear or uniform.

_____ _____
(pueblo/ciudad)   (fecha)

¡Hola! / Querido / Querida _____ ,

Muchas gracias por tu carta. Estoy encantado(a) de haberla recibido.
Espero que todo te vaya bien.

Yo vivo en un / una _____ . Hay _____
                               (tipo de casa)

habitaciones. Hay _____ , _____ ,
_____ y _____ .

Yo tengo mi propio cuarto. / Yo comparto mi cuarto con
_____ . En mi cuarto, hay
_____ , _____ y _____ .

También tenemos un jardín / balcón con
_____ .

¡Escríbeme pronto y descríbeme tu casa!

¡Adiós! / ¡Hasta pronto! / Tu amigo(a),

_____
(tu nombre)

 © Sinéad Leleu, Belén de Vicente Fisher and Brilliant Publications

_____
(town/village)

_____
(date)

Hello / Dear _____ ,

Thank you for your letter. I was delighted to get it.
I hope you are well.

I live in a / an _____ . There are _____ rooms.
                    (type of house)
There is _____ , _____ , _____
and _____ .

I have my own bedroom. / I share my bedroom with
_____ . In my bedroom, there is _____ ,
_____ and _____ .

We also have a _____ garden / balcony with
_____ .

Write soon and describe your house!

Bye! / Talk soon! / Your friend,

_____
(your first name)

Vocabulario adicional
Extra vocabulary

un sótano	a basement
una cocina	a kitchen
un salón	a sitting-room
un dormitorio	a bedroom
una oficina	an office
un cuarto de juegos	a playroom
un baño	a bathroom
un ático	an attic
un garaje	a garage
un comedor	a dining room

mi hermana	my sister
mis hermanas	my sisters
mi hermano	my brother
mis hermanos	my brothers

grande	big
pequeño(a)	small
una flor	a flower

los columpios	swings
un árbol	a tree
una anilla de baloncesto	a basketball ring

una cama	a bed
una mesilla de noche	a bedside table
una tele	a TV
una televisión	a television
un armario	a wardrobe
una alfombra	a rug
un reproductor de CD	a CD player
una cómoda	a chest of drawers
un póster	a poster
una estantería	a set of shelves

una casa	a house
un apartamento	an apartment
una caravana	a caravan
una casa flotante	a houseboat

Puntos adicionales
Extra points

1. Plurals

If you have more than one of a certain room or piece of furniture, do not forget to make the noun plural. For example:

Hay un dormitorio.	There is 1 bedroom.
Hay 4 dormitorios.	There are 4 bedrooms.

Hay un póster.	There is a poster.
Hay pósters.	There are posters.

© Sinéad Leleu, Belén de Vicente Fisher and Brilliant Publications

2.1 or a

The number '1' and the word 'a' are both translated into '*un*' or '*una*', so

There is 1 bedroom.

There is a bedroom.

} Hay un dormitorio.

There is 1 television.

There is a television.

} Hay una televisión.

¡Ideas adicionales!

Extra ideas!

Include a photo or drawing of your house or apartment block.

Mi dormitorio (my bedroom) / Mi dormitorio ideal (my ideal bedroom)

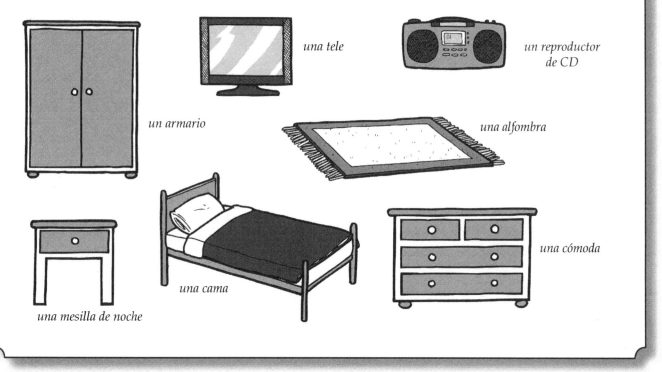

un armario

una tele

un reproductor de CD

una alfombra

una mesilla de noche

una cama

una cómoda

_____   _____
(pueblo/ciudad)   (fecha)

Querido / Querida _____ / ¡Hola!

Gracias por tu carta. / Me puse muy contento(a) al recibir tu carta.

Espero que estés bien. Yo estoy bien /muy bien / genial.

A mí me encanta/ A mí me gusta la Navidad. ¿Y a ti?

En _____ muchas familias celebran la Navidad.
     (tu país)
Los niños dejan sus calcetines en la chimenea y Papá Noel les deja

regalos.

En el día de Navidad ceno con _____ . Comemos

_____ . ¿Y tú? Después de cenar, tiramos de los

'crackers'.

Esta Navidad, me gustaría _____ . ¿Y a
                                                        (un regalo)
ti?

¡Feliz Navidad y Próspero Año Nuevo!
Tu amigo(a),

_____
                (tu nombre)

© Sinéad Leleu, Belén de Vicente Fisher and Brilliant Publications

_____
(town/village)

_____
(date)

Dear _____ ,

Thank you for your letter. / I was very happy to get your letter.

I hope you are well. I'm fine / very well / great.

I love / I like Christmas. How about you?

In _____ many families celebrate Christmas. The
(your country)
children leave stockings on the chimney. Father Christmas leaves
presents in them.

On Christmas Day, I have dinner with _____. We
eat _____ . How about you? After dinner, we pull
'crackers'.

This Christmas, I would like _____ . How about
(a present)
you?

Merry Christmas and Happy New Year!
Your friend,

_____
(your first name)

Vocabulario adicional
Extra vocabulary

Nochebuena	Christmas Eve
un belén	the crib
un árbol de Navidad	a Christmas tree
los adornos	decorations
las guirnaldas	tinsel
una estrella	a star
un regalo	a present

en Inglaterra	in England
en Irlanda	in Ireland
en Escocia	in Scotland
en Gales	in Wales

un monopatín	a skateboard
un juego de ordenador	a video game
un ordenador	a computer
un CD	a CD
un teléfono móvil	a mobile phone
una bici (bicicleta)	a bike
unos patines	roller blades
un libro	a book
un DVD	a DVD
un juego de mesa	a board game

el pavo	turkey
las patatas asadas	roast potatoes
las zanahorias	carrots
las coles de Bruselas	Brussels sprouts
un 'mince pie' (un pastel de frutas)	a mince pie
un pudding de Navidad (tarta con pasas y ron)	a Christmas pudding

mi madre	my mother
mi padre	my father
mi hermana	my sister
mi hermano	my brother
mis abuelos	my grandparents
mis primos	my cousins

Puntos adicionales
Extra points

1. Christmas cards

In Spain, some people send Christmas cards, but they aren't as popular as in the United Kingdom.

2. Stockings for Santa?

In Spain, children don't leave out stockings at Christmas. On the 6th of January, Spanish people celebrate Kings Day (Reyes). Children leave out water and food for the three wise men (kings) and their camels. They leave a shoe for the three kings to fill up with presents.

3. Crackers

Pulling crackers is not a Spanish tradition.

Spanish Pen Pals Made Easy
© Sinéad Leleu, Belén de Vicente Fisher and Brilliant Publications

¡Ideas adicionales!

Extra ideas!

Although sending Christmas cards isn't as popular in Spain as it is in the United Kingdom, you could make a card to send to your pen pal. Write a greeting such as:

Feliz Navidad y Próspero Año Nuevo
(Merry Christmas and Happy New Year)

As most Spanish people don't usually know about Christmas crackers, you could make one for your pen pal. You will need:

◆ a toilet paper tube
◆ crêpe paper
◆ a ribbon
◆ goodies such as sweets, a paper hat, a small toy

Don't put a snapper in as it is illegal to post them overseas.

Instructions:

◆ Fill the tube with some goodies.
◆ Wrap the tube in the crêpe paper.
◆ Gather the crêpe paper at both ends of the tube and tie with the ribbon.
◆ As your pen pal may not know what to do with the cracker, include the following instructions:

> *Dos personas cogen cada uno de un lado y tiran. La persona con la mayor parte se queda con el regalo.*
>
> (Two people hold an end each and pull. The person with the biggest piece gets to keep the content.)

_____   _____
(pueblo/ciudad)   (fecha)

Querido / Querida _____ / ¡Hola!

Gracias por tu carta. Me encantó tu carta. ¡Muchas gracias!

Las vacaciones de verano van a llegar. _____ !

Cuando pienso en las vacaciones, pienso en _____ ,
_____ y _____ . ¿Y tú?
¿En qué piensas?

En _____ , me voy a
     (mes)
_____ con
    (país o ciudad)
_____ / me voy a casa para relajarme.
¿Y tú? ¿Te vas de vacaciones?

También voy a _____ .
    (haz una actividad)
¿Tú qué vas a hacer este verano?

Hoy hace _____ . ¿Qué tal está el tiempo por ahí?

¡Escríbeme pronto!
¡Hasta pronto! Tu amigo(a),

_____
(tu nombre)

Spanish Pen Pals Made Easy
© Sinéad Leleu, Belén de Vicente Fisher and Brilliant Publications

_____
(town/village)

_____
(date)

Dear _____ / Hi!

Thank you for your letter. / I loved your letter. Thank you!

The summer holidays are coming. _____ !

When I think of the holidays, I think of _____ ,
_____ and _____ . How about
you? What do you think of?

In _____ , I'm going
(month)
_____with
(to a country/ a town)
_____ / I'm going to relax at home.
How about you? Are you going on holiday?

I'm also going to _____ . What are you
(do an activity)
going to do this summer?

Today, it's _____ . What's the weather like over there?

Write soon!
Talk soon! / Your friend,

_____
(your first name)

Vocabulario adicional
Extra vocabulary

¡Fenomenal!	Great!
¡Fantástico!	Fantastic!
¡Maravilloso!	Wonderful!
¡Yupi!	Yippee!

ir a un campamento de verano	to go to a summer camp
una colonia de vacaciones	a holiday camp

la playa	beach
el sol	sun
levantarse tarde	to lie in
un castillo de arena	sandcastle
el mar	sea
un picnic	picnic
un helado	ice cream

jugar al fútbol	to play football
jugar al baloncesto	to play basketball
ir a clases de español	to go to Spanish classes
ir a montar a caballo	to go horse riding
jugar juegos	to play games
ir de camping	to go camping

mi familia	my family
mis padres	my parents
mis abuelos	my grandparents
mis primos	my cousins

hace buen tiempo	it's fine
hace sol	it's sunny
está lloviendo	it's raining
hace calor	it's hot
hace frío	it's cold
hace viento	it's windy

Puntos adicionales
Extra points

1. Exclamation points and question marks
In Spanish the exclamation points and question marks are put in twice, once at the beginning and then at the end. The punctuation at the start of the sentence is upside down. This is often forgotten.

2. When does 'tu' need an accent?
When 'tu' is used to refer to a person (for example: ¿Y tú? How about you?), there is an accent on the 'u'. However, if 'tu' is referring to 'your' (for example: tu carta), the 'tu' does not need an accent as it is does not refer to a person.

Spanish Pen Pals Made Easy

¡Ideas adicionales!

Extra ideas!

Include a map of Europe. Use arrows to point to countries you would like to visit:

Aquí están los países que me gustaría visitar.
(Here are the countries I would like to visit.)

If you have visited some of these countries, you can say:

Aquí están los países que he visitado.
(Here are the countries I have visited.)

© *Sinéad Leleu, Belén de Vicente Fisher and Brilliant Publications*   *This page may be photocopied for use by the purchasing institution only.*

Printed in the United Kingdom
by Lightning Source UK Ltd.
133557UK00001B/10/P